ORTONA
STREET FIGHT

ORTONA
STREET FIGHT

MARK ZUEHLKE

RAVEN BOOKS
an imprint of
ORCA BOOK PUBLISHERS

Library and Archives Canada Cataloguing in Publication

Zuehlke, Mark
Ortona street fight / written by Mark Zuehlke.
(Rapid reads)

Also issued in electronic format.
ISBN 978-1-55469-398-6

1. Ortona, Battle of, Ortona, Italy, 1943. 2. Canada. Canadian Army.
Canadian Infantry Division, 1st--History. I. Title. II. Series: Rapid reads
D763.182077 2011   940.54'215713   C2011-900328-7

First published in the United States, 2011
Library of Congress Control Number: 2010943298

Summary: A dramatic account of Canada's first major triumph of World
War II—the December 1943 battle for Ortona, Italy.

*Orca Book Publishers is dedicated to preserving the environment and has
printed this book on paper certified by the Forest Stewardship Council®.*

Orca Book Publishers gratefully acknowledges the support for
its publishing programs provided by the following agencies:
the Government of Canada through the Canada Book Fund and the
Canada Council for the Arts, and the Province of British Columbia through
the BC Arts Council and the Book Publishing Tax Credit.

Design by Teresa Bubela
Cover photograph courtesy of Library and Archives Canada
Frederick Whitcombe, NAC, PA-163411

ORCA BOOK PUBLISHERS   ORCA BOOK PUBLISHERS
PO Box 5626, Stn. B   PO Box 468
Victoria, BC Canada   Custer, WA USA
V8R 6S4   98240-0468

www.orcabook.com
Printed and bound in Canada.

14 13 12 11 • 4 3 2 1

CHAPTER ONE

They had numbered about sixty at dawn. Now just seventeen still stood. The others had been killed or wounded. The survivors faced the hundred yards of open ground where the company had been butchered. Twice they had tried to cross it. Twice they had stumbled through the mud, firing from their hips, screaming defiance. Twice they were forced back by the same drenching German fire that had cut down their comrades.

Beyond that open stretch of land stood the outskirts of Ortona. Between lay abandoned vegetable gardens and olive trees so

1

torn by shellfire that they looked like twisted fenceposts. A tight row of two- to three-story buildings faced the open ground. Explosions had shattered all the windows. Enemy paratroopers were using the openings to snipe at the Canadians. More snipers were on the rooftops or dug in at the base of the buildings. Still more paratroopers hunched behind machine guns, MG42s, whose rate of fire was so fast each long burst sounded like someone ripping a sheet in half.

The Canadian dead lay scattered in the open, broken toy soldiers in wool khaki uniforms. Most lay facedown, arms stretched ahead of them. They had died running toward the buildings. The survivors hated leaving the dead where they had fallen. But it had taken all of them just to bring out the wounded.

In a few minutes Lieutenant John Dougan expected to join the dead, for he was about to lead the men in another charge. Dougan thought it madness. His company commander agreed.

Major Jim Stone had said as much into the radio handset. But the battalion commander on the other end had told him to get on with it.

Stone, Dougan and the company sergeant major had then huddled in a ditch running with muddy rainwater. Stone decided only a third of them would attack. The others would fire everything they had from the ditch. They would try to make the Germans duck from their guns. Stone was a fair man and brave as a lion. He broke a match into three lengths, dropped them into a helmet, and each man drew a piece. Dougan never won gambles. His was the short one.

* * *

"Can you lay down some smoke to cover us?" he asked. Private Elwyn Springsteel said he could see the German machine-gun positions. He and his loader would blind the enemy with smoke bombs from the company's two-inch mortar.

That would help. But Dougan still thought he and the six men going with him would die. He desperately searched for a way to reach the buildings that did not require crossing that open ground. *Then he saw the ditch.* Narrow. Barely three feet deep. From the deep ditch where they huddled, it ran across the open ground to a large apartment building. If they hunched over and ran up it single file, maybe the Germans wouldn't see them. Unless they had a machine gun aimed up the ditch.

Dougan had been fighting Germans for six months. He and the rest of 1st Canadian Infantry Division had landed in Sicily on July 10, 1943. They had fought their way across the island as part of the British Eighth Army. Then they had crossed onto the toe of mainland Italy and marched up its craggy boot. Now it was December. They found themselves in this muddy hellhole on the Adriatic coast. Ortona stood roughly parallel to and east of Rome. Italy's capital was the prize they marched toward.

Dougan had noticed earlier that the Germans expected the Allied troops to be logical. And logic said a rifle company should advance across open ground in sections spread out over a wide front. This was supposed to create too many targets for the defender to deal with. Some were bound to survive to overrun the defensive positions. Stone's 'D' Company had tried to do this twice already. Going up a ditch in a bunched-up line was illogical. So Dougan was going to gamble that the Germans would not be prepared for it. Or so he hoped. "Hell, we're all going to die anyway. Might as well give it a go," he said.

* * *

As Springsteel fired his mortar for all it was worth, Dougan dashed up the ditch with six men hot on his heels. He expected to hear the horrible ripping sound of the machine gun and to die. But not a shot was fired. He and his men piled out of the ditch. Pressed against

5

the hard brick wall of the apartment building, they gasped for air. They were both sweating and shivering from the cold. And dripping wet from the icy drizzle falling. Dougan turned to signal Stone to bring the rest of the company forward. But the big major was already coming out of the ditch with the others right behind.

Seventeen men were now behind the German positions. They looked at the paratroopers huddling in their gun pits. The men in coal-bucket helmets still peered out at the open field, calmly waiting for the Canadians to appear like ducks in their shooting gallery. Stone grinned fiercely. "Nobody but a bunch of madmen would have attempted that dash," he said.

But the madmen had dashed and now they could win. Dougan wrenched a door open and the company filtered quickly and quietly through the empty building. They looked down upon the Germans from upstairs windows. Rifles, Bren guns and Thompson submachine guns fired as one. The Germans died where they were.

There were other Germans, however, in Ortona. In fact, Ortona was lousy with troops of the 1st Parachute Division. 'D' Company of the Loyal Edmonton Regiment had only won a toehold inside the place. Now, on December 21, the true battle for Ortona began.

CHAPTER TWO

War came to Ortona for no special reason. It was just a small town in the wrong place. Ortona stood on a cliff overlooking the sea. Some claimed it had been founded in the thirteenth century BC by Trojans fleeing the fall of Troy. Regular earthquakes had erased any trace of these ancient origins. The oldest remaining structure was the castle. It stood on the high point at the north end of town. Also battered by earthquakes, the castle's thick sandstone walls were slowly collapsing down the cliff. Close by, the great dome of Cattedrale San Tommaso rose high above the other buildings.

Most of the town's old sector was about five hundred years old. Its buildings were usually two- or three-story-high row houses built of brown brick. A stout wooden door provided access to the single large room on the ground floor. This room had originally been used as a shop by a craftsman or merchant. Living quarters occupied the upper stories. Brightly painted wooden shutters covered the upper windows that opened onto narrow wrought-iron balconies.

Like most Italian towns, Ortona had several Roman Catholic churches. San Tommaso was the largest. But there was also San Francesco. It stood in a square on the east side of the town. This square was also home to the town's hospital and school.

Ortona's oldest church was Santa Maria di Constantinopoli. Its foundation stones dated back to the fourth or fifth century AD. But the upper structure had been replaced after an earthquake in the medieval age. This plain little church backed onto a steep embankment on the town's southern outskirts.

* * *

Ortona was surrounded by cliffs and steep banks. The highest and steepest was the cliff that faced the sea. A broad, cobblestone esplanade ran along the clifftop. When siesta ended in the late afternoon, the esplanade was a popular gathering place for the townspeople. They strolled, chatted and enjoyed the stunning seaside view from the wide walkway.

The esplanade looked down on a narrow strip of ground set between the cliff and the sea. Two tunnels had been cut into the base of the cliff at the northern end of the town. Digging them had further undermined the foundation of the castle and sped its collapse. But the tunnels were necessary to allow trains to reach the small harbor.

Ortona's harbor was not sheltered by natural formations. The coast here was wide open to storms. To create an artificial shelter, two long and narrow walls had been built by dumping rock and earth into the sea. These moles, as they were called, projected far out from the shore. At their outer tip they almost joined. Boats could come and go from the harbor through the narrow gap between. The moles resembled a crab's extended claws.

The harbor provided a safe port for the town's many fishermen and the occasional freighter. A sheltered beach was crowded with racks on which the fishermen dried their nets. Most of the fishermen lived in Ortona. At the end of each day, they faced a thirty-minute climb up flagstone stairs that zigzagged up the cliff face to the esplanade. Fishermen did not have the money to pay to be whisked up on the gondola. That was for the wealthier tourists who flocked to Ortona each summer. They would arrive by train, board the gondola and be swept high over the heads of the fishermen and poorer tourists trudging up the stairs.

Tourists came for the sun and surf. They slept in Ortona, but they spent their days on the wide sandy beach south of the town. It stretched almost four miles to where a headland jutted out into the sea. The Moro River emptied into the sea near the center point of the beach. This minor stream had cut a deep ravine into the clay soil. It required a brisk half-hour's walk along narrow dirt roads to go from the Moro River to Ortona. Between river and town one walked through olive groves and vineyards. There were a few farmhouses scattered about. But many farmers lived in Ortona or the hamlets on the edge of the Moro River. Each morning they walked out to tend their fields.

* * *

The fishermen, farmers and other residents of Ortona were mostly poor. This was one reason the town had changed little since medieval times. Most of the cobblestone streets were still so narrow an ox cart could barely pass through.

The back alleys were an even tighter squeeze. A couple of men walking together would brush shoulders.

Ortona's poverty had only worsened since the war began in 1939. Many men had been drafted into the army or navy. Italy's military paid poorly and with no regularity. This meant families back home received little money and often none at all.

In May 1943, the Allies had destroyed the last remnant of the German and Italian armies in North Africa. The invasion of Sicily had come on July 10. Fifteen days later, Italy's fascist leader, Benito Mussolini, was deposed. A new government was proclaimed and began negotiating the country's surrender to the Allies.

Germany's response was quick. In just five days thousands of troops flooded into Italy. The former ally was reduced to another of Germany's occupied countries.

A small garrison of Germans arrived in Ortona. They immediately began forcing the remaining local men and teenage boys to work for them. These men had to dig fighting positions around the town and across the plain to the Moro River. In front of these positions, they strung barbed wire and planted mines. Nobody liked helping the Germans. Many men and boys attempted to avoid being rounded up. They hid or engaged in dangerous cat-and-mouse games with the Germans. They would slip from house to house, often on improvised catwalks extending from one window to another. Those caught trying to escape were sometimes shot. More often they were sent to Germany as slave laborers.

Things got worse when the Allies started advancing up the Italian boot. Refugees began to arrive from the south. Soon the town's population soared to about ten thousand. Many of these were housed in the dark and windowless rooms on the ground floor of the old section's buildings.

While most of Ortona was very old, there was a newer part on the southern edge. It consisted of some modern houses, warehouses and a few apartment buildings. These were separated from the old quarter by scattered farms and other little clusters of houses. Several roads ran from these newer areas to an intersection in a plaza on the southern edge of Ortona proper. The roads converged on a street called Corso Vittorio Emanuele that ran directly through the center of the old part of Ortona to a plaza in front of Cattedrale San Tommaso.

John Dougan and his six madmen had won one of the apartment buildings in this new part of Ortona, a small victory that opened the way for more Canadians to begin advancing. Within the hour the Eddies, as the Loyal Edmonton Regiment was nicknamed, and their comrades from the Seaforth Highlanders of Canada were pressing up various roads that led toward Corso Vittorio Emanuele.

The paratroopers gave ground grudgingly, and only after men on both sides had been killed or wounded.

The Germans could not stop the Canadians reaching the plaza on the edge of the old quarter. They had to fight the Eddies and Seaforths across too broad a front. There were not enough paratroopers to defend every possible line of advance. They tried to establish fighting positions that enabled them to overlap lines of fire. But there were so many low stone walls, dense vineyards, irrigation ditches and clusters of houses that small groups of Canadians could slip between the German positions. Once they got behind or alongside the Germans, the Eddies and Seaforths fired with deadly effect on the German defensive positions.

The Germans kept falling back toward the old quarter. That was fine with the Canadians. They expected to gain its outskirts by evening. Then they would dig in and wait for the dawn. When the sun came up on December 22, the Germans would probably have quit Ortona under the cover of darkness. The paratroopers were unlikely to make a stand in the narrow streets among those ancient buildings.

CHAPTER THREE

Allied intelligence officers did not expect the Germans to defend Ortona. There was no reason to do so. Instead the paratroopers would likely retreat a short distance to the north and dig in on the bank of the Arielli River. This is what the Germans usually did. They made the Allies fight for each river crossing and defended the approaches to towns. They rarely offered more than a token fight in a town itself.

Both sides tried to avoid street fighting, especially in the narrow, twisting streets of ancient Italian towns. There was no way for commanders to control events in such fighting.

Troops became scattered through the buildings. Small clusters of men ended up fighting battles in isolation from everyone else. Supporting arms could not be brought to bear effectively. The tanks could hardly move along the streets and were too vulnerable to anti-tank weapons. Artillery could not be accurately directed against enemy targets. Most of the time the enemy was so close that artillery was as likely to hit its own men as the enemy. Such friendly fire was always a danger on a battlefield. But it became almost inevitable when soldiers fought inside a town.

The battle became a slugging match between infantry. Soldiers would have to take one house after another by breaking in on the defenders. Then it was a close-quarters brawl fought with rifles, submachine guns, grenades, bayonets and fists. There was no way to predict the outcome. And there was always another house just beyond. Both sides were certain to suffer heavy losses in such fighting.

That was why it was avoided. That was why Allied intelligence officers had assured the Canadian general commanding 1st Canadian Infantry Division that the Germans would not stand inside Ortona. And that was what Major General Chris Vokes had told his men.

* * *

Believing the Germans would not try to hold Ortona was not the first mistake that led to this battle. Things had gone badly wrong from the outset of Eighth Army's late-autumn offensive. General Bernard Law Montgomery had launched the operation on November 25. He had vowed to deal the Germans a "colossal crack." His army would charge up the Adriatic coast to the small city of Pescara. It would then swing inland via a valley that led directly to Rome. The Italian capital would be his before Christmas. The Germans would then quit Italy entirely.

British Prime Minister Winston Churchill had declared Italy key to attacking Europe's "soft underbelly." Montgomery intended to deliver a fatal punch that would open the way for an Allied advance into the heart of German-occupied Europe from the Mediterranean.

Monty was a small whippet of a man. He had a thin, reedy voice. But it was a voice that carried when he made speeches. Monty gave a lot of speeches. He liked being close to his troops, to have them see him and hear his intentions. Monty would arrive in a car and jump onto the hood of a jeep or the turret of a tank. His uniform would be rumpled. He would wear his trademark tanker's beret. Not that Monty had ever commanded an armored corps unit or ridden into battle inside a tank. The soldiers gathered around and listened eagerly as he described how they were going to beat the Germans and send them running. If the men were Canadians, he would call them "my Canadians." The New Zealanders were "my New Zealanders." The Indian troops were equally "his."

And they were his. For British Eighth Army was British only in name. Within its ranks marched Canadians, New Zealanders, Sikhs and Hindus from India, Englishmen, Irishmen and Scots. The Canadians were newcomers to its ranks. Eighth Army had come into being in North Africa in September 1941. It had been the army that had finally booted the German Afrika Korps out of Africa after almost two years of bloody campaigns. Only in July 1943 did 1st Canadian Infantry Division and 1st Canadian Armored Brigade join the Eighth Army. They came from England to participate in the Sicily invasion.

* * *

The Canadians won the respect of the rest of the army in Sicily. They also earned German respect. The paratroopers gave 1st Canadian Infantry Division its nickname. They declared the Canadians "The Red Patch Devils." The nickname was inspired by the small red rectangle of cloth that each 1st Division soldier wore on the shoulders of his uniform. Each Canadian division had been assigned a different badge color. Another shoulder patch bore the word *CANADA*. A third indicated his regiment. The three badges instantly identified a soldier's nationality, division and regimental assignment.

"We see the Red Devils coming and we fire our mortars hard. But the Red Patches just keep running through the fire," a captured paratrooper told Canadian Press reporter Ross Munro. "I can't understand it. Other troops we fought lay down and took shelter when the mortars fired right on top of them. The Red Patches are devils. They keep on coming." Munro quoted the man in a newspaper story. And the legend of the Red Patch Devils was born.

About seventeen thousand Canadians wore the red patch. Less than half were infantrymen. These were the men who went head-to-head

in combat with the enemy. They were sometimes called the division's teeth and sometimes
the sharp end. The job of the rest of the men
was to help the infantry fight.

Everyone agreed that the infantry had the
most dangerous job. They were several times
more likely to get killed or wounded than
anybody else. Not that those soldiers in other
jobs never faced danger or became casualties.
There were artillerymen who went forward
with the infantry to call in firing targets over
their radios. Men in the engineer companies
often had to build bridges, repair roads and
lift enemy mines while under fire. Medical
personnel went onto the battlefield carrying
stretchers or in jeep ambulances to evacuate
the wounded. Quite often these men became
casualties themselves. There was nowhere in a
division that was really safe. A German artillery
or mortar round could kill a man anywhere he
served. And every job was essential to enabling
the division to fight.

One thing infantry divisions lacked when going into a fight were tank regiments. These armored regiments were organized into separate entities that were then attached to the infantry division. The tanks supporting 1st Division were grouped in 1st Canadian Armored Brigade. About 3,500 men served in the three tank regiments that made up the armored brigade. It fielded about 200 tanks.

CHAPTER FOUR

The Canadians were in reserve when Montgomery launched his "colossal crack" on November 25. The British 78th Infantry Division and 8th Indian Division led the advance. Montgomery had expected the German Fifth Army to give way easily. Instead Field Marshal Albert Kesselring rushed fresh divisions to meet the Eighth Army at the Sangro River.

This river was about twelve miles south of Ortona. Montgomery had expected to cross it quickly. He would then advance across the Moro River, pass by Ortona on its inland side and dash to Pescara, about fifteen miles north of Ortona.

It was barely thirty miles along the coast from the Sangro River to Pescara. Montgomery had hoped to cover the distance in a few days. Instead 78th Division lost 4,000 men, killed or wounded, crossing the Sangro and reaching the south bank of the Moro River. Covering the eight miles between took the British troops a full week. Montgomery realized the division was too worn out to continue fighting.

So the torch passed to the Canadians. On December 4, 1st Division and 1st Armored Brigade set up on the south bank of the Moro River. The Moro flowed through a narrow, steep ravine. All bridges over the river had been blown. The Germans were dug in on the opposite bank. The Canadians could seldom see any movement. The enemy was hidden in fortifications camouflaged with vegetation. Other Germans were hiding inside the build- ings of the little hamlets standing on the edge of the ravine. The enemy artillery, mortars and tanks were concealed farther back. But these weapons could all range in on the Canadians.

German artillery and mortars rained shells down. The Canadians were also fired on by the six-barreled launcher the Allied troops called "Moaning Minnie." Its nickname came from the ear-piercing shriek the shells made as they fell like a clutch of explosive eggs.

* * *

The Loyal Edmonton Regiment took up a position to the rear of its sister regiments on December 4. Out front were the Seaforth Highlanders and the Princess Patricia's Canadian Light Infantry. These regiments formed the 2nd Canadian Infantry Brigade. It was one of the division's three brigades. The nine regiments in these brigades gave the division its fighting teeth.

Each brigade came from a distinct part of Canada. Most of the men in 2nd Brigade's

Loyal Edmonton Regiment were from northern Alberta. The Seaforths came from Vancouver and the British Columbia interior. Because the Patricia's was a Permanent Force regiment, whose men remained on army payrolls during peacetime, its members hailed from all over the western provinces.

Each brigade had one Permanent Force regiment. The 1st Brigade's was the Royal Canadian Regiment. Its men were mostly from Ontario. And the soldiers in the brigade's other two regiments came from two distinct parts of this province. The 48th Highlanders were Torontonians, while the Hastings and Prince Edward Regiment drew men from the central Ontario farm country.

Quebec and the Maritimes manned 3rd Brigade. Its Permanent Force regiment was the Royal 22e Regiment from Quebec City. The Carleton and York Regiment was formed in New Brunswick, and Nova Scotians filled out the ranks of the West Nova Scotia Regiment.

* * *

Ortona was clearly visible from the southern bank of the Moro River. Edmonton scout platoon leader Lieutenant Alon Johnson noticed how the great dome of the cathedral stood out in the midst of its surrounding cluster of old buildings. The dome shone as if coated in brass.

Johnson was twenty-three. He and Lieutenant John Dougan had enlisted together in Edmonton on March 25, 1942. They had been attending the University of Alberta. They were also cadets in the Canadian Officers Training Corps. Three of their friends joined them over the next few days. One scrubbed out in the early stages of officer training, but the others had earned the rank of lieutenant and been posted to the Edmonton regiment overseas.

It was during the Sicily invasion that these young men began to take command of Edmonton rifle platoons. Each got their command after the man who had been leading the platoon was either killed or wounded. That was what being a reinforcement meant. You came up to a unit to replace men who had fallen.

Johnson only got a platoon at the end of the fighting in Sicily. But Dougan and his close friend Earl Christie had got theirs in the middle of the campaign. Christie had been in medical school at the University of Alberta. Dougan and Johnson considered him the brightest of them all. They believed he was destined to have a brilliant medical career. He would probably find a cure for cancer or some such thing.

* * *

On August 5, Christie and Dougan had led their men in a desperate charge up a barren Sicilian hillside. It was known only as Hill 736. This was its height in meters. They should have gone into the attack with seventy-two men— thirty-six to each platoon. But more men had been lost than could be replaced. So Dougan and Christie attacked with just forty-three men between them.

The artillery had fired shells ahead of their advance up the steep slope. This was called a creeping barrage, and the idea was to stay right behind the exploding shells. The Germans were supposed to duck into their slit trenches to escape the shellfire. They would start coming out once the shells rolled past them. But the Canadians would be on top of them by then.

That was the theory. Sometimes it worked. Other times it was impossible to keep up with the shells. Dougan, Christie and their men did okay on that front. They were no more than a couple of hundred yards behind the exploding rounds. That was so close that bits of stone, clods of soil and shards of steel shrapnel flew all around them as they clawed their way upward. But things went to pieces when the barrage swept over the summit.

Dougan looked up and saw men in coal-scuttle helmets jumping into position behind a row of machine guns. They were yelling and sounded mad as hell.

A hell-storm of fire ripped into the Edmontons. Christie fell, dying. Splinters from a bullet that shattered his rifle pierced Dougan's arm. Another slug penetrated his helmet. It whirled around inside like a mad bee before exiting out the back side. Blood started gushing from a cut on his forehead. Half blinded, Dougan managed to draw his pistol. Gripping it in both hands, he blundered up onto the summit with a handful of men. They took the hill in a bloody gunfight. Dougan lived, Christie died. It could have easily gone the other way. There were times Dougan thought it should have. His friend Christie's grand potential was squandered on that barren Sicilian hillside.

CHAPTER FIVE

The Canadians kicked off the attack across the Moro River on December 5. A cold rain fell on the opening day of what would eventually be called the Battle of Ortona. But this was not yet a fight for the town. The objective was still to go past Ortona.

That remained the case as the days ground on and the Canadians made little progress. Six days were spent just getting across the Moro. Then it took another two days to fight through to a point marked on topographic maps by a narrow little line. This line was about a kilometer south of Ortona. It ran straight from the sea toward the mountains. Not until the Canadians reached the spot did they realize that it was far more than a little line on a map. They faced a deep, narrow gully.

The Germans had dug deep holes into the southern bank that protected them from the Canadian artillery fire. When the shelling stopped, the Germans dashed up to the gully's edge and started firing their machine guns. The ground the Canadians attacked across was open. It also sloped up toward the gully's edge. So the Germans fired down on them, just as if they were on a hilltop rather than inside a gully.

The Canadians quickly started calling the position "The Gully." It was a mark of respect. It was where one Canadian regiment after another was chewed up and spit out by the Germans.

By this time the weather had completely soured. Drenching rain turned the clay soil into a mire of mud. The wet clay gummed onto the men's boots so that it looked like they ran forward on snowshoes. But these snowshoes consisted of ten or more pounds of thick, gooey mud. It was impossible to brush off. They had to scrape it away with bayonets or olive tree branches. Such branches were everywhere. The olive groves had been blown to pieces by fire from both Canadian and German artillery. It was the same with the vineyards. Deep shell craters were everywhere. Farm buildings had been smashed to ruins. Repeatedly the Canadians attacked, only to be thrown back.

* * *

The Royal 22e Regiment broke the deadlock on December 14. The legendary Van Doos managed to turn The Gully's inland flank. In Quebec, the French Canadian population was lukewarm to the war and strongly opposed conscription. Yet each Canadian division overseas had one regiment of French Canadian soldiers. Most of these men were from Quebec.

All of the eighty-one soldiers from 'C' Company were French Canadian. Captain Paul Triquet led his men into the attack at 7:00 AM. The thirty-three-year-old headed straight for a large farmhouse called Casa Berardi that lay two kilometers away. His men and the tanks were right behind. Artillery officer Captain Bob Donald was alongside Triquet, using his radio to call down a wall of fire on either side of the advancing force and out to its front.

The Canadians advanced inside this protective cloak of steel and blast. But even so, men fell with every step. Noon found the company still well short of the farmhouse with only thirty men still in the fight. All Triquet's platoon officers had fallen. They were surrounded by German paratroopers. Only the heavy fire from the Canadian Sherman tanks and the artillery kept the enemy at bay.

"The safest place is the objective," Triquet cried. He then led his men forward. Triquet repeatedly jumped onto the lead Sherman to point out targets he wanted destroyed. Bullets struck all around him. Triquet ignored the danger. "They can't shoot. Never mind them! Come on!" he shouted.

Suddenly Casa Berardi was there amid the smoke and flames. A final dash and the survivors cleared the farmhouse and outbuildings in a short, sharp fight. Only four tanks were still with them. The others had been knocked out by German fire. 'C' Company numbered just fourteen. They barricaded doors and windows. The tanks crowded in close to the main farmhouse. Infantry and tankers threw back one counterattack after another. Shrapnel from an exploding shell sliced Captain Donald's body almost in two.

The battle raged through to midnight. Finally more Van Doos managed to get through to bolster Triquet's numbers. The German paratroopers eventually slunk off into the darkness. Triquet's heroism at Casa Berardi was rewarded with a Victoria Cross. This was the highest military honor for bravery that could be awarded to a Canadian.

Seizing Casa Berardi enabled the Canadians to get behind the defenders holding The Gully. They also cut a road that ran between The Gully and Ortona. This road served as the main German route for supplying troops fighting south of Ortona. The Germans now had no choice but to retreat before they ran out of ammunition and fresh troops.

Not that the Germans gave up easily or quickly. They stopped trying to regain Casa Berardi on December 15. But they did not withdraw from The Gully entirely until December 20. Most of the paratroopers were then seen pulling back into Ortona itself. To the Canadians it seemed the Germans were planning to retreat to the north by going through the town. They did not realize that the paratroopers had been using the past few days to fortify Ortona.

CHAPTER SIX

Intelligence officers at 1st Canadian Division's headquarters were delighted when The Gully fell. "The enemy is likely to fall back... abandoning Ortona and making his next stand on the line of the Arielli," they predicted. Major General Vokes passed the good news to 2nd Brigade's Brigadier Bert Hoffmeister. All his Loyal Edmontons and Seaforth Highlanders had to do was gain the town's outskirts. The Germans would then quit the town.

The delay in driving the Germans back from the Moro River had forced Montgomery to abandon hopes for winning Rome before Christmas.

Every day it rained harder, and the region's rivers were swelling and widening. This made bridging them ever more difficult. The deepening mud was also hampering the movement of tanks and heavy trucks. Winter had settled on Italy, and now there would be no major advances until spring.

But Montgomery would be able to say he had won Ortona. The town was not strategically important, but it would be useful as comfortable winter quarters for his army. His intelligence staff predicted that the port could soon be used. All his supplies were currently being landed on Italy's boot heel and then trucked to the army—an army advancing steadily away from this landing site. With the capture of Ortona, supplies could be landed right on the army's doorstep. All Eighth Army had to do was fix the damage the Germans had caused to the harbor to prevent its use. This consisted of many vessels sunk inside the harbor and gaps blown in its protective moles.

Montgomery's staff predicted the Germans would withdraw behind the Arielli River by December 24. Eighth Army would be able to have a peaceful Christmas. And many of them would be able to enjoy Christmas in the dry, warm comfort of Ortona's houses.

* * *

The notion that Eighth Army would spend a pleasant Christmas relaxing in Ortona would have amused the German paratroopers. They were busily preparing to roll out a welcome mat for the Canadians. It would be a welcome mat from hell.

Years of constant combat had ground 1st Parachute Division down. It was under-strength, and many new recruits were poorly trained. But the paratroopers still considered themselves to be elite soldiers.

Germany's parachute divisions fought with the regular army. Yet they were not part of it. They were part of the Luftwaffe,

Germany's air force. In the early years of the war the paratroopers had become famous for their combat jumps on enemy targets and their ability to fight and win against the odds. There were still veterans of those glory days.

Fritz Illi was a platoon commander with a rank equal to Company Sergeant Major. He was one of the old originals. Illi had been eighteen when Germany invaded Poland in September 1939. His entire high school class in a town near Stuttgart had enlisted for military service. Illi had immediately requested to try out for the parachute divisions.

On May 10, 1940, his parachute battalion had ghosted out of the sky onto a Dutch airfield at Rotterdam. That had been his first combat jump. Since then, there had been seven others. Among these was a jump as part of the German airborne invasion of Crete. In the early morning hours of May 20, 1941, almost all of Germany's paratroopers were dropped on the island in the eastern part of the Mediterranean. The paratroopers took terrific casualties. Many were killed before they could get untangled from their parachutes. Illi was hit by a mortar fragment. It left his little finger dangling by a string of sinew. A medical officer simply sliced the finger off, slapped on a bandage and sent him back into combat. Illi fought for another fourteen days until Crete was won. The Germans had dropped close to 30,000 paratroops on the island. About 2,000 were killed, over 2,000 wounded and another 2,000 reported missing. The men in the last group were believed either killed or lost as prisoners. Illi walked away from Crete a hardened survivor.

By December 1943, combat jumps were a thing of the past for the paratroopers. Many recruits were no longer even trained in parachuting. The parachute divisions had been blended into regular army formations. While they no longer trained for airborne jumps, the paratroopers were still highly trained combat soldiers. Every man in 1st Parachute Division thought he stood among Germany's finest.

* * *

Illi had not been involved in the fighting at The Gully. He had been in Ortona, preparing that welcome mat. He and his men had been doing so since December 12. For eight days they prepared to meet the Canadian attack on the town. They took dynamite and blew houses apart to create piles of rubble. Then they dug fighting positions deep inside the ruins. Illi would carefully check each position to ensure the men in it would enjoy a good field of fire toward the Canadian line of advance. Once satisfied, he would move his platoon to another area. More buildings would be blown up and more fighting positions created.

Soldiers from the division's engineering companies worked around Illi's platoon. They laid mines all through the rubble. The mines were positioned to protect the fighting positions Illi's men created. The engineers were clever and skilled. Some were veterans of the great Russian Front street battles in Leningrad and Stalingrad. Those cities had devoured thousands upon thousands of soldiers from both sides. The German army had suffered terrible defeats in both.

The veterans of Stalingrad and Leningrad taught the other engineers their tricks. A functioning toilet could be turned into a trap by hooking an explosive charge to the plunger. If a Canadian thought to enjoy relieving himself on a real, functioning toilet, he would be in for a surprise. The moment the toilet flushed, the detonator cord attached to the handle triggered the explosive. And blew the bathroom to pieces.

Bottles of wine were set invitingly on tables or in cupboards. Invisible line connected the bottle to explosives hidden from sight. Pick up the wine and *bang!* The engineers considered such explosive traps good pranks. Extremely deadly pranks. They had many tricks in their bags. There were mines that blew off a foot when stepped on. Mines that popped a couple of feet into the air when triggered and spit deadly steel pellets into the guts of the man facing it. Italian box mines were popular. Metal detectors could not find these wooden mines. They could be buried in rubble to look just like a small board. Such a board would offer good footing. But stepping on it closed the mine's wooden lid and detonated the explosives.

CHAPTER SEVEN

When the Germans started preparing Ortona for a street battle, they tried to force the residents to leave. The people were given no time to gather possessions. They were just ordered to go. Many did. But just as many refused to go. Some hid in the warren of the back streets. Others took refuge in the railroad tunnels that cut under the castle in the town's northern corner. A smaller number escaped toward the Canadian lines. Some warned that the Germans were creating much destruction within the town. The civilians did not realize that the Germans were destroying things to make it easier to defend Ortona. They mistook the acts for simple vandalism intended to make the place uninhabitable.

By December 19, all the narrow side streets were blocked with rubble from destroyed buildings. Two large buildings were blown down that morning to block the Corso Vittorio Emanuele at the entrance to the square that faced Ortona's town hall. A huge pile of rubble completely plugged the street. It stood taller than a man and as wide as a couple of trucks parked beside each other. The engineers quickly dug mines into the pile. Other soldiers set up machine guns and anti-tank guns.

Across the plaza from the rubble pile, the municipal hall was topped by a small tower with a clock mounted in it. The Germans removed the clock. This left a large, round opening at the top of the building. Sandbags were manhandled into the tower to create a protected firing position. Then a heavy machine gun was set in place. Through its sights a paratrooper could zero in anywhere along the length of Corso Vittorio Emanuele.

The Cattedrale San Tommaso had another clock tower built alongside it. The tower had been built in the medieval age. In the 1920s, its height had been increased so that it could serve as a military observation post. At dawn on December 21, the engineers set off a large amount of dynamite at the base of the tower. The collapsing tower sliced the cathedral's dome in half like a sharp knife carving a melon.

* * *

The cathedral dome was smashed at about the same moment Lieutenant John Dougan and his six madmen had made their bold dash into Ortona's outskirts. A few minutes later they had been reinforced by the rest of the Loyal Edmonton's 'D' Company. Major Jim Stone's small band of soldiers had then ambushed from behind the paratroopers guarding the edge of the town. The rest of the regiment dashed forward to secure the tenuous toehold the company had won.

'C' Company of the Seaforth Highlanders soon came up to the right of the Edmontons. Its men had climbed the steep embankment that the small church of Santa Maria di Constantinopoli backed onto. Again the Canadians succeeded by doing something unexpected. The embankment was steep and heavily overgrown by dense brush. Climbing it was slow work. The Germans had left it virtually unguarded because they expected the Canadians to come up the road that switchbacked up to the town's outskirts. But the Seaforths ignored the road and scrambled up the embankment. And took the little church. The Germans set up to defend the road now found Canadians on either side of them. They had no choice but to pull back in order to escape being surrounded.

But they did not go far. The paratroopers were determined to make the Canadians fight for the town's outskirts. It gave more time for the engineers and other paratroopers working inside Ortona's heart to create defensive positions.

* * *

Now that the road was clear, several Sherman tanks ground up to join the Seaforths. The tanks were from the Three Rivers Regiment. The Shermans arrived just in time. Captain Don Harley had led off the Seaforth attack with 'C' Company just after the church had been taken. The men had moved along a road running from the church toward an intersection with Corso Vittorio Emanuele at the southernmost square. The road was initially bordered mostly by low stone walls that protected small gardens and olive groves. As it drew closer to the square, the agricultural plots were replaced by interlinked rows of two- and three-story houses.

Harley's men had just reached the first of these housing clusters when they met stiff resistance. Everyone scattered into the olive groves

and took cover. Harley kept trying unsuccess-
fully to rally his men and get them advancing
again. But every time a man showed himself,
the paratroopers lashed out with heavy fire.
'C' Company started taking heavy casualties.

The tanks tipped the scales in the Seaforths'
favor. One Sherman, with the name *Cobourg
II* scrawled in white paint on its gun turret,
squatted square in the middle of the street.
Its heavy 75-millimeter main gun punched
shell after shell down the length of the road to
smash up one target after another. Soon, spent
brass cartridges lay in a ragged pile behind the
tank, as the loader threw the empty shells out
of a hatch.

This fire cracked the German defenses, and
Harley's 'C' Company got moving. The tanks
rumbled along behind. Whenever German
resistance stiffened, the Shermans pounded
their positions with shells.

Things continued to go well until the
Seaforths were just short of the square and

the entrance to Ortona's old quarter. As the buildings along the road grew more numerous and closed in on them, Harley's men met ever stronger German positions.

Harley tried sending men up side roads to get behind the Germans. They soon came back, reporting that these streets were dangerously narrow and blocked by large piles of rubble from demolished buildings. Some piles were fifteen feet high. When a man tried climbing one, he was immediately fired on by a sniper or machine gun.

At 11:00 AM, Brigadier Bert Hoffmeister received matching reports from the Seaforths and Loyal Edmontons. Both were meeting fierce resistance and had not yet reached Ortona's old quarter.

* * *

Hoffmeister was a popular brigadier. He had joined the Seaforths as a boy cadet in the early 1930s and worked his way up through

the ranks. By the time of the Sicily invasion, he commanded the regiment. He was
promoted to command 2nd Brigade soon
after the landing on the Italian mainland. Yet
Hoffmeister was not a professional soldier. He
was a militiaman who had held a regular job
during the week and soldiered on weekends.

Canada's Permanent Force was always
small in peacetime. It was intended to form the
backbone around which the militias provided
the flesh and muscle. The volunteers serving as
part-time soldiers in the militia regiments gave
Canada the ability to field an army quickly.
And it was men like Hoffmeister who led these
militia regiments into battle.

Hoffmeister was no fool. He recognized
now that the Germans were not going to
give up Ortona without a fight. Up to this
point the Edmontons and Seaforths had
been advancing just a couple of companies
toward the square. Hoffmeister decided he
would have to commit the entire brigade to

clearing the town. He ordered the Seaforth and Edmonton commanders to send their entire strength into the battle. The Princess Patricia's were held back because there was not enough room for three regiments to fight side-by-side within the town's narrow confines. More Three Rivers tanks were called up.

The Canadians had been avoiding firing artillery at Ortona, hoping to save it for Eighth Army's use as winter quarters. But Hoffmeister and Major General Vokes agreed the time had come to take off the gloves. Now the gunners directed their 25-pounder artillery pieces at Ortona. As one, the guns roared and spat shells down on the town. More buildings were smashed into rubble. The Germans were also raining artillery and mortar fire down upon the areas that had been cleared by the Canadians. With every passing hour, more of Ortona was systematically reduced to ruin.

* * *

By nightfall on December 21, the Edmontons and Seaforths had pushed through to the edge of the square. Up ahead, the Corso Vittorio Emanuele ran off into the heart of the old quarter. The two regiments settled in for the night. The men would rest and prepare to renew the fighting at dawn.

The tanks rumbled off to locations well back of the front lines. They were too vulnerable and exposed at night to remain in Ortona's narrow streets. It would be easy for raiding parties of paratroopers to creep up on a tank and knock it out with shoulder-launched anti-tank weapons called *Panzerfausts*.

In Ortona there was no clear front line. Germans and Canadians were often directly opposite each other. Some actually occupied different parts of the same house. Moving in the darkness was dangerous. The men standing guard on both sides were jumpy and tended to fire at the slightest sound or movement.

Both sides were realizing the price of getting tangled in a street fight. Companies on both sides had been whittled down to about half their normal strength. The Seaforths had set up their regimental head-quarters in Santa Maria di Constantinopoli. By the light of a candle, the regiment's intel-ligence officer wrote in the daily war diary that he was shocked by the losses Harley's 'C' Company had suffered. Its men, he wrote, were "busy burying their own and enemy dead. The company's casualties being seven killed and many wounded." The Seaforths were down to just 524 men. Normally they numbered about 850.

On the other side, Corporal Carl Bayerlein was more exhausted than he ever remembered being. He was one of the engineers. Bayerlein had spent most of the day laying mines and setting explosive traps inside houses. In the late afternoon, his platoon had finished that job and taken up positions on rooftops of houses looking out on the square. They had sniped at the advancing Canadians with their rifles.

"As soon as we were spotted the enemy brought in tanks," Bayerlein wrote in his personal diary. "These fired shells until the buildings fell. The only possibility of escape was to jump on to the other roofs of adjacent buildings. The enemy artillery is constant and falls everywhere in the city. The visibility was limited because of the dust of the explosions and houses collapsing." With nightfall, Bayerlein's platoon moved into the basement of a pharmacy and collapsed into a dreamless sleep.

CHAPTER EIGHT

A bold dash. Another madman's gamble. Major Jim Stone believed he knew how to smash through 1st Parachute Division's defenses along Corso Vittorio Emanuele. Obviously the German demolitions in the side streets were designed to confine the Canadians to the main route through the center of Ortona. The tactic was working because Brigadier Bert Hoffmeister had ordered the Loyal Edmontons to do just that on the morning of December 22. But Stone knew that going straight up the street would get his men slaughtered.

John Dougan's mad dash up the ditch had worked. So why not do the same thing on a grander, more daring scale. Wasn't the Corso rather like a ditch?

The Germans would again expect the Canadians to be logical. To cautiously advance, clearing each house on either side of the street as they went. And the paratroopers would make them fight for each bloody house. That kind of house-to-house fighting would just chew the Edmontons up.

Stone knew the Germans were out there waiting. They would be concentrated on the Corso because logically the Canadians had to go up it. Yet they would not be able to leave the other streets unguarded. So they would have been forced to spread out across the entire width of Ortona. It was the only way to prevent the Canadians slipping men behind them. If the Germans were spread out like that, then they were stretched across the town like a thin rubber band.

So, do the unexpected. Charge right through the Germans defending the Corso. Snap the rubber band in two. Give the paratroopers no time to pull back to a new defensive line. His Eddies would dash through to the other end of town. They would stop for nothing.

All he needed was some tanks to accompany them. The tanks could lead. They could shoot up anything in their way. Blast the buildings with their guns as they rumbled past. And the Eddies would be running alongside and behind. It was daring. Precisely the kind of crazy stunt the Germans would never expect. They would be thrown off kilter. Given no time to recover. Stone would have completely outflanked them. The paratroopers would have no alternative. With his men behind them and the rest of the Edmontons and Seaforths bearing down from the front, they would have to run. Right out of Ortona. A costly street fight could be avoided.

Stone found his tanks. "Let's start at first light," he told their commander. "You put your tanks in low gear. Get your sirens going. Fire your main armament at every building forward of you and your machine guns at the houses on the side of the road. I'll put my infantry alongside the tanks and let's try and go through."

The tanker didn't like the idea. But Stone kept talking. He wore the man down with words and won that battle.

* * *

Major Stone set about winning the battle for Ortona at dawn. The Three Rivers sent Shermans from No. 2 Troop forward, with Stone's 'D' Company alongside. Two other companies of Edmontons were close behind. Normally a regiment had four companies. Losses the day before had been so high that one company had been disbanded. Its men bolstered the strength of the other three. Each company still had only about sixty men.

With four full companies the Edmontons normally numbered more than four hundred.

The tank sirens and the thunder of their 75-millimeter guns firing in the narrow street struck Stone as "terrifying." They headed for the next square along the street. It was called Piazza Municipali. The square was no more than three hundred yards distant. The buildings on either side of the street were hundreds of years old. At the entrance to the square, the huge rubble pile blocked the street. The municipal hall stood behind the pile. Stone could see there was a gaping hole where the clock should have been. The shattered cathedral was visible beyond the square and the crumbling castle farther back. Stone could see it all. Could see the entrances to the tangled streets where they would have to fight house-to-house if the gamble failed.

But he was winning. The Germans were letting the tanks and infantry pass. Barely a shot fired. Stone thought the paratroopers must be frozen by fear and confusion. They were closing on the rubble pile. It stood at least twenty-five feet high. But the debris was scattered so that it was like a gently rising hill. Stone thought the tanks could scale it. Tanks and men could cross together and then dash to the castle.

Twenty-five yards left now. And the lead tank suddenly stopped. The other tanks halted like ducklings waddling after their mother. The tankers quit firing. Stone's infantry started milling. The men had no idea what was happening.

Stone leaped onto the hull of the lead tank. Shouted into the open hatch at the crew commander, "What the hell's the matter?"

The man poked his head out and pointed at a thin scrap of sheet metal lying in front of the rubble pile. "It's probably concealing a mine," he said.

Bricks, stones, chunks of metal, broken boxes, glass and other debris from the battered and destroyed buildings lay strewn along the entire length of the street. So why did this bit of sheet metal mean anything? Stone demanded. The commander refused to budge. Stone argued. He was standing on the side of the tank. Stone would be one of the first targets if the Germans woke up and opened fire. But the big man stayed put. Arguing and cajoling. Trying to put some backbone into the tanker. Who explained that his tank cost about twenty thousand dollars and that he was not going to risk it being damaged.

Stone felt the attack's momentum slipping away, like grains of wheat trickling between his fingers. "You armored sissy," he snapped. "I've got twenty to thirty men here with no damned armor at all. They're worth a million dollars apiece. You're just a bunch of goddamned armored sissies."

* * *

The Germans woke up. Bullets started snapping around the Edmontons, and the men dived for cover. Then a small anti-tank gun started cracking rounds at the tanks. It was positioned on a corner by the cathedral. The tankers were unable to get the angle to return fire.

Stone yelled at his PIAT man to take the damned thing out. A PIAT was the anti-tank launcher used by Canadian infantry. PIAT stood for Projector Infantry Anti-Tank. It was a hand-held weapon that weighed thirty-two pounds and fired a 2.5-pound hollow-charge explosive bomb. The thing was difficult to load, prone to breakdown, complicated to operate and generally unpopular. Stone was hardly surprised when the PIAT man fired and the round sailed harmlessly over the armored shield that protected the Germans manning the anti-tank gun. The soldier started the slow task of reloading.

Stone was in a total rage. He knew that any moment the Germans were going to score a killing shot on one of the tanks. He chucked a smoke grenade in front of the anti-tank gun. Smoke began curling up and blinding the German gun crew. Stone was too angry to give sensible orders. He just charged alone toward the gun while he pulled the pin on a fragmentation grenade. Stone stopped inches from the gun shield and flipped the grenade over it. The explosion killed the gun crew.

Stone stalked back to his men and the tanks still stalled before the rubble pile. He kicked the metal sheet to show there was nothing under it but cobblestone. Lieutenant John Dougan pointed to two Edmontons who had clambered over the rubble pile. They were creeping carefully toward the municipal hall. Suddenly one fell dead, and Dougan called the second man back.

The tankers were going nowhere. If his men crossed the rubble pile alone, they would be caught in the open and killed. Stone and Dougan told their men to batter down the doors to the houses on either side. It was time to get to work. Time for the house-to-house fighting to begin. Stone had gambled that with the tanks he could bull right through Ortona. He had lost.

CHAPTER NINE

Stone and the other Canadian officers in Ortona lost control of the fighting within minutes. The men became too scattered through the buildings and side streets. Sergeants, corporals, even privates took charge. The Canadians had no real experience in street fighting. Nor had they been trained for the task. To stay alive, they had to learn the job on the fly.

Three German machine guns fired from a building next to the rubble pile. Private Charles Gordon Rattray and two other men set their sights on knocking them out. They crawled over the rubble pile on their stomachs. Machine-gun slugs and rifle bullets fired by snipers on the rooftops struck all around the men. Somehow they reached the building unharmed.

Rattray kicked in the front door and dashed inside. He shouted over his shoulder for the others to clear the main floor while he pounded up the stairs. Rattray broke into one upstairs room and killed the Germans manning a machine gun there. He then moved to the next room and the one beyond. His attack was so quick, the Germans didn't realize Rattray was there until he started shooting. He eliminated the three machine guns in a matter of seconds. Five Germans surrendered. The rest he killed. Rattray was awarded a Military Medal for valor.

Silencing these machine guns was one of the few Canadian successes during the day's fighting. A number of buildings were captured. But the Edmontons failed to advance beyond the rubble pile.

Private Melville McPhee's experience was typical. The twenty-one-year-old from Drumheller had developed ulcers during the Sicilian campaign. This day only made them worse. Dodging into a building, McPhee headed for the stairs. And saw a stick grenade bouncing down. He dived into a closet just off the stairs as the grenade exploded. Every time McPhee tried to slip out of the closet, another stick grenade came bumping down the stairs. Only the closet protected him from the shrapnel and blast of the next explosion. The German above seemed to have an endless supply of grenades that the Canadians called potato mashers. It seemed hours before McPhee poked his head out without seeing another grenade clattering down. He immediately seized the moment and ran out of the house. McPhee decided the German with the never-ending grenade supply could have the bloody place.

Meanwhile, the Seaforths passed behind the Edmontons to come up on their western side.

This gave the Edmontons responsibility for clearing Ortona from the Corso Vittorio Emanuele over to the esplanade. The Seaforths were to push through a maze of narrow streets to the square containing the school and hospital. There was so much German artillery and mortar fire raining down on them that it took the entire day for the Seaforths to get positioned for their new line of advance.

* * *

The Canadians in Ortona were in a bad way when night fell on December 22. They had suffered many casualties during the past two weeks. Both infantry battalions were at about half their normal strength. These men were scattered throughout the town in small groups. Each little party settled down for the night inside a building or behind one of the many piles of rubble. Their job was to maintain some semblance of a continuous front line. It was a difficult task in the darkness and unfamiliar streets.

To make it impossible for the Canadians to rest, the Germans kept firing machine guns and rifles. Both sides continued to pound the other with artillery and mortar fire throughout the night. The resulting racket was hellish. There was also the constant danger of the paratroopers creeping up to attack their positions. So it was necessary for at least half the men in each party to be awake at all times.

Conditions were better for the Germans. They had deployed just one battalion inside Ortona for the day's fighting. It had about as many men as the two Canadian battalions together. These men were well rested. In a street battle the defender always had the advantage. Paratroopers could wait in their prepared positions for the Canadians to come to them. Men watching from the rooftops could follow the progress of the Edmontons and Seaforths and direct others to positions facing them. This enabled the Germans to only commit some of the battalion to the fighting. The others were able to rest in the railroad tunnels. They were safe from the Canadian artillery fire.

The paratroopers were well trained in street fighting. They were used to operating in small independent groups. They were skilled at slipping small parties of men behind the enemy. Once they got inside the Canadian lines, the paratroopers could carry out a lightning-fast raid on a single position. Or they could set up a machine gun and shoot up a large part of the Canadian rear area. Getting a reaction force organized to counterattack the machine gun required at least a few minutes. Before the Seaforths or Edmontons could get moving, the machine-gun crew usually slipped away into the darkness. And struck again at another spot.

CHAPTER TEN

Major General Chris Vokes realized 2nd Canadian Infantry Brigade was now locked in a costly duel with the Germans. He had already provided all the direct support available. The division's artillery was pounding the town. A regiment of tanks had been committed.

What they needed was to break the deadlock. Vokes knew only one way to do that. He had to get men around the north side of Ortona. Surround the town and the Germans in it would have to surrender. Even coming close to surrounding them would work.

These paratroopers were not suicidal. They wanted to live to fight another day. Threatening their line of escape would force them to flee Ortona.

This was the first real fight Vokes had faced as a divisional commander. He had commanded 2nd Brigade in Sicily and been promoted to command the division just before it landed on the Italian mainland. Vokes was a tall man with a temper as fiery as his red hair. He swore more than most soldiers.

His command debut had not gone well so far. Montgomery thought the Canadians took too long getting from the Moro River to Ortona. Yet doing so had cost the division heavy casualties. Many blamed Vokes for the slowness of the advance and losses suffered. Vokes had repeatedly sent single battalions to attack the Germans head-on. The battalion was usually shot up and forced to retreat. Another battalion was then ordered to attack the same spot. One futile attack followed another.

It had been the brigadiers and battalion commanders who figured out how to break each German line. They had men scout out ways to get around the Germans. Threaten their rear. Just like Vokes wanted to threaten the paratroopers in Ortona.

But getting men beyond Ortona was going to be tough. The sea blocked the right side. So the Canadians must go around on the left.

Vokes gave the job to 1st Canadian Infantry Brigade. Its commander was the exact opposite of Vokes. Brigadier Dan Spry had been a Boy Scout leader before the war. He was soft-spoken and almost never swore. Spry hated losing men foolishly. This made him a careful planner.

Spry agreed the Canadians had to threaten the German rear. The question was how to get there. Immediately to the east of Ortona there was a deep ravine. A narrow ridge on the opposite side provided the only viable route. The Germans would expect the Canadians to try advancing along the ridge.

Even moving forward was going to be tough. It rained harder with each passing day. The single dirt road running along the ridge was a mucky mess flanked by vineyards. Tanks were of little use on such ground. His infantry battalions would have to go it alone.

* * *

Spry sent the Hastings and Prince Edward Regiment forward at 9:30 AM on December 23. A squadron of Ontario Regiment tanks gamely accompanied the infantry. Engineers carrying metal detectors walked in front of the tanks. They searched for the inevitable mines. The infantrymen moved through the vineyards alongside the road. They had to hunch over to pass under the highest wire supports and at the same time step carefully over the lower ones. Pushing through one row of grapevines only brought them to another identical row. It was exhausting work. The mud clung to their boots. Rain drenched their wool uniforms.

Artillery fire smashed down in front of the advancing men and tanks. The gunners were trying to drive the Germans to cover.

The advance went well at first. The tanks even kept up. Within sixty minutes the Hasty Ps, as the regiment was nicknamed, had almost reached their objective. This was a small hill about halfway along the ridge. They were to take this ground and hold it until the 48th Highlanders could pass through. The 48th would then carry on to the end of the ridgeline. Which would put them roughly even with the north end of Ortona.

Spry figured that would be the cue for the Germans to leave. The Royal Canadian Regiment would curl around and surround the place if they didn't. The paratroopers inside would then be trapped. And the Canadians would destroy them.

It was a good plan. One that looked like it might succeed, until the Hasty Ps were just a hundred yards from the hilltop. Suddenly, paratroopers began firing machine guns from a string of fortifications running across the hillside. Mortars and light artillery positioned on the other side of the hill zeroed in on the exposed infantrymen and tanks.

The tanks on the road were unable to fire at the German positions. So they turned up a farmer's narrow track to find a better angle. The engineers were still out front. Their detectors were finding one mine after another. Minutes were lost as the engineers dug up and defused each mine. The tanks abruptly halted when they came upon a narrow gully. When the engineers started to go into it, they were driven back by machine-gun fire. The lead tank bulled forward alone and immediately had a track blown off by a mine. That was it for these tanks. They were out of the battle.

* * *

The Hasty Ps had taken cover on their bellies in the muddy vineyards. Bullets ripped through the vines above their heads. Mortar rounds and artillery shells exploded all around.

Lieutenant Colonel Bert Kennedy never hunkered. He strode to the front of the Hasty Ps and began crisply giving orders. Kennedy seemed untouchable. Bullets and shrapnel whizzed harmlessly past. His refusal to shrink from the enemy fire rallied the men.

Slowly they pushed forward. Each platoon of thirty men was broken into three equal-sized sections. Two sections stayed back, firing their guns furiously. This covered the advance of the third section for a short distance. That section then threw out gunfire while another came up to it. These two sections covered the third as it leapfrogged through to a new position ahead.

Over and over the platoons leapfrogged forward this way. By midday, the Hasty Ps gained the hilltop. Thirteen men were killed and more than twice that number wounded. But the paratroopers also suffered heavily.

Many had been trapped inside their fortified positions. The Canadians had killed them with grenades and rifle shots.

Kennedy strolled back and forth on the hilltop as his men dug slit trenches in the mud. "Take it easy, lads," he said. "No matter what happens, we will look after you." The Hasty Ps had done their job. They had taken the hill. They just had to hold it until the 48th Highlanders reached them.

There was a lot of rivalry between these two Ontario regiments. Because the Hasty Ps were mostly central Ontario farm stock, the Highlanders called them "Plough Jockeys." "Glamour Boys," the Hasty Ps wisecracked back. It was mostly in jest. The men in either regiment would lay their lives on the line for the other.

CHAPTER ELEVEN

It was a day of brutal fighting in Ortona. The Seaforths advanced into the narrow maze of streets on the west side of the town. Their objective was the square with the hospital and school. The Eddies continued trying to get past the large rubble pile in front of the plaza dominated by the municipal hall clock tower. Men moved into the streets to the east to look for a way past the municipal plaza. Other troops began pushing up the esplanade.

The Germans resisted fiercely. Paratroop platoon commander Fritz Illi moved his men constantly from one hot spot to another.

Illi was exhausted. He had never seen such awful fighting. There was no letup. The platoon would occupy a firing pit in a rubble pile or inside a house. Then they would open fire on the Canadians. Who fired back. A couple of his men would die or be wounded. The Canadians would close in. Illi would pull the platoon back before it was overrun. And the process began again somewhere else.

Both Canadian battalions gained a little headway every hour. But only by a house or two. Tanks were of little use. The streets were too narrow and strewn with mines. Eddies pushed two six-pounder anti-tank guns up the Corso Vittorio Emanuele by hand. They used the guns as building-busters. The first shot fired was armor-piercing. This was a shell intended to penetrate a tank's armor. It easily punched a large hole in a building's outer wall. The crew then pumped high-explosive shells through the hole. These rounds tore deep into the building before exploding. The explosive blast and shrapnel spray of one round inside a house caused great destruction. Firing five or six rounds into a building in a matter of seconds turned the rooms into killing zones.

Seaforth Company Sergeant Major Jock Gibson led a small section from 'D' Company up a street. They advanced single file. Each man pressed up close to the buildings on one side. The man out front dashed forward and ducked into a doorway. Then the second man leapfrogged past to the shelter of an alley. He was quickly passed by the third man. Soon the last man in line was out front. They gained a total distance of perhaps twenty yards each time they hopped forward this way.

Gibson was so bloody tired. His uniform was caked in mud mixed with blood from fallen comrades. He stank of gunpowder and sweat. Whiskers rasped his hand when he wiped a cheek. A bath would be heavenly.

He looked across an intersection and saw a Seaforth officer and two men. They approached the door of a building. The officer raised a rifle. Gibson realized he was going to bash the door open with its butt. "Watch out!" he yelled. "Don't touch that door." Too late. The door cracked open and an explosion threw the officer into the street. Gibson ran to him. The officer's ankle was hanging loose. Only a small scrap of flesh and muscle linked it to his leg. Gibson bandaged the ankle and leg together. Then he carried the officer back to the medical-aid post at Santa Maria di Constantinopoli church. He delivered the man and explained that the officer had triggered a hidden explosive. Then Gibson walked back toward the never-ending battle.

* * *

Loyal Edmonton Captain Bill Longhurst was sick of watching men die in the streets. But there was no safe way to advance. Longhurst had been thinking. Looking at the rows of connected houses, he realized that using the streets was a fool's game. It was playing according to German rules. Putting themselves right in the enemy's scopes. So the thing to do was advance *inside* the buildings.

Each battalion had a platoon of men trained as explosives specialists. They were called pioneers. Longhurst had the Edmonton pioneers tie several bricks of plastic explosive together. The big bomb was then carried to the top floor of a house. He dragged a chair up against the outside wall, and the pioneers set the bomb on it. There were Germans in the house on the other side of the wall.

Longhurst gathered a small force of men on the lower floor. The pioneers set the explosive fuse burning and tumbled down the stairs. They had just hit the ground floor when the charge exploded. "We all tore up the stairs to get through the mouse-hole before the dust subsided, but there was no hole." They had blasted aside one wall and now stared at a second wall. Longhurst and the pioneers set to work preparing another charge.

This time the men dashed through the smoke and dust in the room to find a gaping hole in the wall. The first section hurled a few grenades through. After these exploded, one or two men jumped into the smoke- and dust-filled room and raked it with Thompson submachine-gun fire. Any paratroopers in the room died before they could react. The next section then moved out. An upstairs floor was cleared by spraying the stairwell with automatic weapons and charging up before the Germans could respond. Downstairs floors were subjected to showers of grenades thrown down the stairwell and then a mad rush by troops firing submachine guns and Bren guns. It was a bloody and dangerous business. But better than moving along the open streets.

Longhurst called the tactic mouse-holing. He put it to good use in a long afternoon of mayhem. Blowing his way through one wall after another, he cleared an entire block of houses. Longhurst noticed something strange during this advance. The Germans in buildings on the other side of the street were withdrawing without a fight. So he was winning both sides of a street while fighting for only one.

* * *

Mouse-holing spread like lightning through Ortona. The Seaforths added their own twist. Seaforth pioneer Sergeant Harry Rankin and his men had recovered a great horde of German Teller mines. These anti-tank mines were shaped like a covered cooking pan. They were about two inches deep and fifteen inches across. Each mine was packed with high explosive that could smash a tank's track and disable it.

Rankin decided Tellers were ideal for mouse-holing. He jabbed a bayonet into the wall and hung the mine from it, slipped a short fuse onto the built-in detonator, lit it and ran like hell. The result was a nice hole ripped through the wall.

It didn't always go smoothly. Sometimes the mine failed to open a hole. Or the explosion brought the whole building crashing down in a thunder of brick and wood. Some officers were peeved when Rankin accidentally destroyed the house they had planned to capture.

Rankin didn't care. He was a tough little guy from the wrong side of the Vancouver tracks. "We aren't exactly practicing scientific demolitions here," he growled.

The destruction he was causing in Ortona didn't bother him either. There was a job to do, so he did it. If a tank was having trouble getting around a tight corner, Rankin's explosives widened the gap. Destruction on demand, he called it. Nothing sophisticated about the methods either. All a Seaforth had to do was send word and Rankin's team appeared to work explosive magic.

General Bernard Law Montgomery (right) considered Major General Chris Vokes little more than a "plain cook" as a military tactician. (ALEXANDER STIRTON, NAC, PA-132783)

Loyal Edmonton riflemen fire on three Germans crouching in a slit trench one hundred yards away during the fight on Ortona's outskirts. (T. ROWE, NAC, PA-163935)

Canadian troops move past the burned wreckage of a German self-propelled gun toward the front lines at The Gully. (T. ROWE, NAC, PA-166562)

Two Loyal Edmonton soldiers help two wounded comrades reach the Regimental Aid Post at San Leonardo. (FREDERICK WHITCOMBE, NAC, PA-114487)

West Nova Scotia Regiment Private Edmund Arsenault mans a PIAT in a slit trench near Ortona. (ALEXANDER STIRTON, NAC, PA-153181)

First Canadian Infantry Division commander Major General Chris Vokes (left), 2nd Canadian Infantry Brigade commander Brigadier Bert Hoffmeister and 1st Canadian Armored Brigade commander Brigadier Bob Wyman in conference during the Moro River–crossing phase of the battle. (T. ROWE, NAC, PA-131064)

'B' Company of the Loyal Edmonton Regiment advances into Ortona on December 21. (T. ROWE, NAC, PA-116852)

Loyal Edmonton troopers advance into Ortona. Lance Corporal W.D. Smith (far right) is carrying a #18 wireless set. (T. ROWE, NAC, PA-163932)

A truck and jeep burn in Ortona after being hit by German mortar fire. A Bren carrier stands in the foreground. (T. ROWE, NAC, PA-170291)

A Seaforth Highlander killed by a sniper while moving through a vineyard on the outskirts of Ortona, December 20, 1943. (T. ROWE, NAC, PA-141302)

Two German paratroopers surrender to the Canadians at the edge of Ortona. (T. ROWE, NAC, PA-107934)

Seaforths and some Three Rivers Regiment tankers (those wearing coveralls) having Christmas dinner in the courtyard of Santa Maria di Constantinopoli.
(T. ROWE, NAC, PA-152839)

Cattedrale San Tommaso after its destruction. (T. ROWE, NAC, PA-136308)

Men of the Loyal Edmonton Regiment rescue Lance Corporal Roy Boyd from the rubble of a destroyed building. Boyd was buried for three-and-a-half days. (T. ROWE, NAC, PA-152748)

On December 23, Three Rivers Regiment tanks push up Corso Vittorio Emanuele toward the rubble pile at Piazza Municipali. (T. ROWE, NAC, PA-114028)

A young woman hangs out washing in the ruins of Ortona on January 13, 1944. (T. ROWE, NAC, PA-114040)

* * *

The Canadians occasionally discovered civilians hiding in buildings they won. Seaforth Captain June Thomas had just cleared the ground floor of a house when an old woman dressed all in black poked her head out of a cellar door. She beckoned for Thomas to follow her into the depths. He went cautiously. He feared a trap. But she led him into a dark, dank room lit only by candlelight. The woman handed him a steaming mug of tea. Several children stared with big eyes from the shadows. Thomas found the scene oddly restful. The candles, the children, the warming tea and the wrinkled smile of the old woman.

Outside, the war waited. Gulping the tea, he handed the woman the mug. Then he ran back up the stairs. Closed the door firmly to protect those below. And went back to being a destroyer.

Ortona was being torn apart. The air was choked with smoke and dust. Fires burned in the wreckage of buildings. There was the constant din of explosions. Machine guns rattling, rifles cracking and masonry collapsing. Nightfall brought no end to the violence. The two sides were deadlocked, and there was no end in sight.

CHAPTER TWELVE

It was almost completely dark when the 48th Highlanders passed through the front line on the ridge held by the Hasty Ps. The Highlanders walked in single file. They numbered about four hundred. They carried only rifles, Bren guns, Thompson submachine guns, ammunition, grenades and a few rations. All the heavy equipment had been left behind. They walked past in silence. The darkness and falling rain swallowed them. As the last man disappeared, one Hasty P muttered to his friend, "Good Christ! The Glamour Boys have gone crazy."

Once again the Canadians were trying a daring gamble. The Highlanders were going to follow a meandering trail in total darkness. It was a trail that had shown up on aerial photographs. At least it appeared to be a trail. Aerial photographs were not always reliable.

Normally the Highlanders would have sent scouts out to make sure the trail was there and led where they wanted to go. Such scouting took time. Major General Chris Vokes was in too much of a hurry. He wanted the Highlanders to advance that very night. Advance to the far end of the ridge. So that was what they set out to do.

The vineyards on either side of the path were a sea of mud. But farmers had probably used the trail for centuries to come and go from their fields. Their footsteps had hardened the path's surface.

The Highlanders would face disaster if the Germans guarded the trail. They hoped

the rain had driven the paratroopers to shelter.
It was a faint hope.

Their pace was slow. It was so dark, each
soldier clutched the bayonet scabbard of the
man ahead. Four hundred men advanced in
one slithering line. Major John Clarke led.
It was impossible to see the path. He had to
feel his way. When his foot started sinking into
deep mud, Clarke knew he was losing the path.
He walked very carefully. Lowering his boot
slowly and gingerly to find firm footing. One
step, then another.

Rain drenched the Highlanders. But they
welcomed it. The rain was noisy. It masked the
sounds of four hundred men. A foot splashing
in a puddle. The clink of metal made by a
grenade bumping a rifle barrel. Soft curses
when men stumbled and almost fell.

Clarke had smiled confidently as he set off
at the head of the column. It had been a show.
He was deeply worried. The aerial photos had
shown nothing that could be used as markers.

There had just been the path and the vineyards beside it. What if another path crossed
it? He could easily take a wrong turn. Lead the
Highlanders blundering off into the vineyards
to nowhere.

Suddenly Clarke saw a house in the gloom
ahead. There had been no sign of it in the photos.
He halted the column. He then advanced with a
single platoon to check things out. Soon he saw
a German sentry hunkered in front of the door.
A Highlander slipped past Clarke, crept up on
the man and knifed him to death from behind.
The platoon surrounded the house. Then one
section burst through the front door. Fifteen
paratroopers sat around a big table in the kitchen.
Their shirts were open. Weapons leaned against
walls or hung from pegs. The table was cluttered
with Christmas parcels and bottles of wine. The
Germans stared blankly at the dripping, filthy
Canadians. Then two went for their weapons
and died on the point of bayonets. The others
meekly raised their hands and surrendered.

Clarke led the column on. They came to another house. Once again they managed to surprise a party of Germans celebrating an early Christmas. Then he came to a third building. It was empty. The major was no longer sure he was on the right path. He had no idea where he actually was. A runner was sent back. He returned with the battalion's commander and intelligence officer. They looked at their maps and the aerial photos. Lieutenant Colonel Ian Johnston grinned at Clarke. He was not lost. Clarke was right on the spot they had set out for. The Highlanders had gone a mile along that trail. They were at the end of the ridge and had got there without firing a shot. The north side of Ortona stood directly opposite. The paratroopers were now threatened with being surrounded.

* * *

It was an amazing feat. But it left the Highlanders in a precarious position. There was not a friendly soul within a mile. The only weapons they had were the light guns each man carried. And the ammunition they had lugged up on their backs. They could burn through it all in a couple of hours of hard fighting, surrender then being the only alternative. The Highlanders hoped phase three of the plan for 1st Infantry Brigade got going quickly. Before the Germans woke up to the fact they were there.

On Christmas Eve morning the third phase began. A company from the Royal Canadian Regiment started to follow the trail through to the Highlanders. It was daylight and the Germans saw the Canadians coming. Artillery and mortar fire rained down. Eighteen men were killed or wounded in seconds. The advance collapsed.

Getting through to the Highlanders by day was obviously impossible. So the RCR waited and tried again after dark. The Germans were now alert and covering the trail. That meant the Canadians would have to advance across country. Crawl through the mud-soaked vineyards. 'B' Company gave it a try. They wriggled on stomachs across a wide vineyard. Several German machine guns opened fire as they came out on the other side. The company fell back in complete confusion.

A bitter Major General Vokes admitted failure. He lacked the strength to cut the paratroopers off in Ortona. The best he could manage was to push reinforcements through to the Highlanders. Maybe their presence on the ridge would convince the paratroopers to quit the town. That was all he could hope.

The Highlanders had passed Christmas Eve surprisingly peacefully. Patrols had reported Germans digging in all around their position. Yet they never attacked. Not a single artillery or mortar shell was directed at them. No snipers took potshots. It was a welcome reprieve. Sooner or later, though, the Germans would come. Chances of holding out seemed slim.

CHAPTER THIRTEEN

Christmas Eve in Ortona passed much like the previous two days. Brigadier Bert Hoffmeister went in to see what was happening. He was frustrated. There was almost nothing he could do to help the men fighting in town. The Eddies and Seaforths were scattered in small groups. Half were busy mouse-holing their way through blocks of buildings. Hoffmeister couldn't even find out where those men were. He climbed to the upper story of one building to look out a window. All he saw were paratroopers across the way. *If I can see them, then they sure as hell can see me*, he thought. Hoffmeister fled. The building was smashed to bits by German artillery shells seconds later.

He walked out of the town and over to the Edmonton battalion headquarters. Their commander, Lieutenant Colonel Jim Jefferson, was talking to a young officer and a group of reinforcements. He was preparing them to go into the town. Offering advice that might give them a chance of staying alive. Hoffmeister thought the young officer looked totally bewildered.

Ortona gobbled up reinforcements. There was no room in street fighting for mistakes. Few of the men had seen combat before. They did stupid things.

Lieutenant John Dougan watched in horror as the young officer marched up the street toward him. Behind were twenty fresh-faced, clean soldiers. Looking like they were on parade. He tried to wave them to cover. But the German mortars were too quick. Seventeen men fell dead or wounded. They had lasted only a few minutes. Dougan helped evacuate the wounded. Blood drenched his lower legs. The tragedy left him exhausted. He limped off to find Major Jim Stone. To report the loss of the badly needed men.

"What's the matter with your leg?" Stone demanded. Dougan said, "Nothing." "What the hell are you dragging it for, then?"

Dougan looked down and saw a gash in the left knee of his pants. Blood was welling out of the hole. He had thought the blood came from the reinforcements. It was his. Dougan was carried out of Ortona on a stretcher.

* * *

Bit by bit the Canadians kept gaining ground. Not because they outnumbered the paratroopers. They were just too determined. The Eddies and Seaforths were going to win or die. There was no thought of quitting.

Lieutenant Colonel Syd Thomson commanded the Seaforths. He could hardly believe how many men had died in Ortona. The stream of maimed or dying coming into the battalion aid post at the little church was staggering. Scattered through the streets and in the wrecked houses were dozens upon dozens of Seaforth dead. Nobody had time or energy to collect them. German and civilian corpses were also strewn about. Thomson feared the Seaforths would be destroyed winning this battle. But *they would win it.*

Captain June Thomas and 'A' Company made winning a little more possible in the early afternoon. They came up a street and were suddenly looking into the square with the school, hospital and a church on various sides. This was their main objective. Piazza San Francesco. Thomas didn't know its name. His map just showed an open space surrounded by large buildings. In its middle was a dead horse. So the Seaforths named it Dead Horse Square.

The paratroopers were firing machine guns out of the church bell tower. Canadian artillery had blown most of its roof away and there were several gaping holes in the walls. But the tower still stood. And the guns in it controlled the square.

Thomas saw that the school across from the church seemed unoccupied. That struck him as odd. But it also presented an opportunity. So he ordered a section of men to occupy it. The men were reinforcements. Private Gordon Currie-Smith was one. Currie-Smith was twenty-six. He stood barely five feet tall and weighed hardly a hundred pounds. But Currie-Smith was a professional soldier. He had joined the army in the mid-1930s and had been training other soldiers until a few weeks before.

Currie-Smith didn't believe the Germans would just let them take the school. He suspected a trap. But nobody listened when he voiced his fears. He went with a few men.

All they found were classrooms with empty desks, blackboards, books on shelves. A school waiting for teachers and kids. Currie-Smith stayed scared.

An hour later his fears were confirmed. An enormous explosion shook the square. The school erupted in a vast shower of masonry. All that remained was a great pile of debris. But under it all, one man still lived. Gordon Currie-Smith was wedged tightly on all sides by concrete blocks and covered feet to neck in rubble. Miraculously, there was a small space around his face that let him breathe. He could not see the sky. Or move at all. He was buried alive inside the school ruins.

* * *

Paratrooper engineer Carl Bayerlein heard the school explode, saw parts of the building thrown hundreds of feet into the air. "We were able to get under cover before the debris came down on us," his diary entry read. The school might have been one of the buildings his team had booby-trapped. It was hard to remember. There were so many.

The amount of explosives they packed into some buildings was amazing. They would cram every conceivable hiding spot with boxes of dynamite.

There was no shortage of explosives in Ortona. Eventually the paratroopers would have to leave. No reason to leave behind unused dynamite or mines. It was Christmas Eve. The Germans left as many deadly presents for the Canadians as possible.

* * *

But Captain Thomas was furious at the school's destruction. Every attempt to gain control of the square was stopped cold by the machine guns in the bell tower. That made him all the madder. Finally deliverance was at hand. A Sherman tank named *Agnes* managed to get through the narrow streets. Thomas ran over and pointed at the bell tower. "As much as I hate blasting the tower of that church," he said, "I want you to get him out of there."

Corporal Gord Turnbull looked down from the tank turret. "It's Christmas Eve and that's God's house," he commented. Thomas snapped back that there was no other choice. Turnbull had to agree. He ordered a 75-millimeter round fired. The bell tower was torn apart.

The Seaforths dashed across the square and into the church. Paratroopers had sand-bagged a position around the pulpit. Men chucked grenades back and forth. Others blazed away with rifles and automatic weapons. It was a bloody brawl that went on into the night. The surviving Seaforths walked out of the church early on Christmas morning. They had killed every German inside. Hell of a start to the holiday.

CHAPTER FOURTEEN

"May this Christmas Day be as merry as circumstances permit." Major General Vokes finished his day's message to the troops with these words. Not a lot to be merry about. Everywhere the fighting only seemed crueler. Each man's death felt all the more by his comrades. There was plenty of dying this Christmas Day.

The 48th Highlanders on the ridge west of Ortona had been discovered at first light. Paratroopers crowded around their position. Germans sniped with rifles, probed with machine-gun fire. Heavy mortars and artillery pounded the Highlanders. Somewhere in the vineyards the grinding sound of tracks and the whine of engines warned that the Germans were bringing up tanks.

Lieutenant Colonel Ian Johnston knew the Highlanders were too under-gunned to fend off a concerted attack. His men were formed in a tight circle. Their guns pointed in every direction. They tensely watched the vineyards and waited for the paratroopers to come.

But the wireless radio saved the Highlanders. It allowed the artillery officer with them to direct his guns onto the Germans. He brought the shelling in so close that the men firing the guns said they were afraid of hitting the Highlanders. The officer said not to worry. He used the guns to form a perfect circle around the Highlanders. It was a killing circle. One of steel and blast. One that kept the Germans at bay. "Just keep shooting," he told the gunners. "Just imagine we're an island." The gunners kept firing. And kept the Highlanders from being overrun.

* * *

All Christmas Day the Royal Canadian
Regiment tried to fight through to the
Highlanders. One attack after another was
driven back. Only about one hundred and fifty
of the battalion's men were still standing at
nightfall. Major Strome Galloway commanded.
He and Captain Sandy Mitchell decided to cheer
up the worn-out survivors. Mitchell had found
an old mandolin somewhere. He sat down on a
broken chair and Galloway held the radio mike
close. Mitchell knew a few bars of this and that
carol. He strummed a few of "Silent Night."
Then a few from another carol. The men in the
slit trenches could hear the mandolin over the
company radio. Another officer had bought a
little wine and bread from a farmer. He slath-
ered slices of bread with bully beef. Then he
walked through the battalion lines handing a
slice to each man and letting him take a sip of
wine. The soldiers smiled grimly and tiredly.
They took the offering and felt blessed.

* * *

In the little church of Santa Maria di Constantinopoli, the Seaforths were more blessed than any other Canadian front-line troops on Christmas. Lieutenant Colonel Syd Thomson had ordered the stops pulled out to make sure the men got a Christmas dinner. And his quartermaster unit delivered. Somewhere they managed to buy a couple of pigs. Somewhere else they rustled up beer and wine. A feast was prepared.

At 11:00 AM the first company of Seaforths rotated out of the line and back to the church. As one company slipped from the battle, another spread out to cover its position. All the companies eventually came out this way. It was a process that took eight hours. Each company enjoyed a bit more than an hour out of the lines.

On offer was soup, pork with applesauce, cauliflower with mixed vegetables, mashed potatoes and gravy. There was Christmas pudding and minced pie for dessert. And a couple of bottles of beer per man. The church organ had survived, and Lieutenant Wilf Gildersleeve serenaded the men with hymns and carols. Some of the men called for bawdy soldier's songs. *Shut up, will you,* Gildersleeve thought silently. *Carols are the things to sing at Christmastime.* And carols were what the men got.

* * *

For the Eddies there was no sit-down Christmas dinner. Major Jim Stone gulped some normal rations and a cold pork chop that had been brought up from the rear. There were not enough pork chops to go around. And many of the Eddies were too isolated and locked in relentless battle to receive a meal.

Little thought was given to its being being Christmas. The Eddies were finally gaining ground. They had got past the square with the municipal hall and rubble pile. Had eliminated the Germans firing machine guns out of where the clock had been removed from the hall.

A short advance had followed. An advance that stalled in front of yet another huge rubble pile. This one blocked the entrance to the next square. On the opposite side of the square was Cattedrale San Tommaso. Stone could see its great shattered dome.

But his men could not reach it. Every square inch of the open square was covered by German machine guns. Stone realized the Eddies were stalling out. He was hardly surprised. His company was down to just thirty men. It was the same for all the companies. Too few men and far too few experienced veterans.

Sergeant J.E.W. Dick was one veteran. His platoon stalled in the face of heavy machine-gun fire. Then the paratroopers started aiming streams of fire at them with a flamethrower. This was the first time they had used this weapon in Ortona. Flamethrowers were terrifying weapons. When the stream of burning fuel jetted onto a man's uniform, it burst immediately into flame. Men burned to death in agonizing pain.

Dick decided to kill the flamethrower operator. He led some men in a dash across an open alley. His goal was a downspout on the side of a building. He and the men went hand-over-hand up the downspout to reach a small room that overlooked the Germans. They shot down on them and forced the Germans back. Dick was awarded a Military Medal.

But the Edmontons remained stuck in front of the square. Private Melville McPhee was close to the rubble pile and hunkered down for the night. A man came up and put two bottles of beer into his hands. He dropped a few slices of cold pork in McPhee's mess tin. He continued on to give others the same portion. McPhee drank the beer and thought it wonderful. He wondered if it might be his last.

* * *

Most of the Germans enjoyed better fare. When not fighting, they rotated back to the safety of the tunnels to sleep. At nightfall a line of motorcycles streamed up to the tunnel entrance with hot food in the sidecars. "We had potatoes, oranges, vegetables, roast beef," a pleased Carl Bayerlein wrote. "We also put up a small Christmas tree."

Bayerlein could not let himself fully enjoy the Christmas spirit. "There is no place for Christmas sentiments here. We do not know how long we can hang on to Ortona."

* * *

On the ridge, the Highlanders received an unexpected Christmas delivery. The Saskatoon Light Infantry provided the division's heavy weapons support. It was they who operated the machine guns, the mortars and anti-aircraft guns that backed up the various infantry battalions. Sixty men from the SLI had volunteered to go up the narrow track during the night and bring supplies to the Highlanders. Each man carried a good hundred pounds of ammunition, rations, spare radio batteries and bombs for the light mortars. They also brought stretchers to carry the wounded out. The men were guided by Highlander Captain George Beal.

They left just after nightfall and by 9:00 PM crept into the Highlander position. A delighted Lieutenant Colonel Johnston told Beal, "You forgot to bring a tank. Ask Brigadier Spry at Brigade to send us tanks, for God's sake." Johnston smiled. "Tell him to send us just one tank and we'll massacre them."

Beal laughed. He asked if Johnston was sure that all he wanted for Christmas was a tank. "That's right," Johnston said. "One Sherman." Beal promised to deliver the message. Then he and the men from Saskatoon headed back on the path with seven full stretchers. Johnston watched them disappear into the darkness and prayed his Christmas wish would come true.

CHAPTER FIFTEEN

At dawn each company commander and his sergeant major huddled together. They counted the men they had left and divided them into small sections. Most were now led by a private or corporal. There were not enough officers and sergeants to go around.

Dawn was the worst time of day for soldiers in combat. A long, frightening night ended with too little sleep managed. It was cold and wet. Another long day of deadly battle ahead. Spirits were at their lowest.

That was when Captain Thomas, Company Sergeant Major Gibson, or Major

Stone slipped in next to them. A kind word. A shake of a shoulder to waken a man. Two canteens offered. One held water. The other dark rum. A swig from either or both was given. The rum helped. It warmed men and helped chase away some of the fear that had grown in the night. Too many men were being sent back because they were unable to stop shaking. Some simply said, "I can't take it," sat down and refused to go on.

The war was back to full fury before the officers finished their rounds. Artillery shells whistled down. Ortona erupted again in fire and smoke. There was the ripping of the German machine guns. The slower, duller thudding of the Canadian Bren guns responding. Grenades popped, rifles cracked. The cannon on the Three Rivers Regiment's tanks boomed. Moaning Minnies shrieked into the Canadian lines. The Canadian anti-tank guns thumped back. Mortar rounds ripped holes in roofs. Explosions sent cobblestones whirring through the streets and tore buildings to shreds. A new day and the battle of Ortona raged on.

* * *

An old woman wandered through Dead Horse Square yelling and raving. Lieutenant Colonel Thomson realized she had gone mad. A shot rang out. The woman fell dead. German snipers stopped any Seaforths from clearing the body away. Then a Three Rivers tank rolled into the square. The tank ground the woman's corpse into bloody mush under its tracks.

* * *

Another tank closed up on the rubble pile in front of the square leading to the ruined cathedral. It was named *Amazing* and commanded by Corporal Joe Turnbull. Joe was Gord Turnbull's brother. Bill was the other brother. All three were tankers in the Three Rivers Regiment. They had enlisted together.

Amazing clawed and chewed its way up onto the rubble pile. It had almost made it over when a paratrooper threw a bomb onto the engine compartment. The explosion set the tank on fire. Joe became separated from his crew when they bailed out. There was so much machine-gun fire hitting around him that he was unable to get back to the Canadian side of the pile. He ran instead to a cellar on the German side and wriggled into it.

Gord Turnbull saw his older brother running. He hammered the German positions with his tank's main gun. When the smoke cleared, there was no sign of Joe. Gord feared he was dead.

* * *

Company Sergeant Major Jock Gibson stared at the reinforcements in front of him. He couldn't believe what they had just said. "What's this?" he bellowed. He thrust a Type 36 fragmentation grenade into their faces.

It was the standard Canadian grenade. The men said they had never seen one before. He held out a rifle. No idea how to clean it, they declared. Gibson grabbed a Bren gun. Never fired one before, they chirped in unison. *Lambs to slaughter*, Gibson thought. *They're sending us bloody lambs who will just get butchered here.* He faced the men and pretended he was on a peace-time parade ground. He held a grenade up. "This is a Type 36 grenade. It has a fuse length of…"

An hour later he sent the men to their fates. He went into an old shack in search of more supplies. The door was closing behind him when what seemed like a dozen German shells exploded just outside. Gibson threw himself under a table. The room seemed to blow apart. He was amazed to crawl out of the ruin without a scratch.

Gibson was shaking. He could not stop the shaking. He realized he was a nervous wreck. "None of us are going to get out of Ortona alive," he muttered.

* * *

Major General Vokes was thinking the same thing. He met with Brigadier Hoffmeister. "Would you like to quit, Bert? Would you like to pull out of Ortona?"

Hoffmeister answered instantly. They had been told Ortona was important. That's why the battle had been started. To pull out now would be to admit that all these men had died or been wounded for nothing. "Besides," he said, "we're winning. I think we should end it."

Vokes looked long and hard at Hoffmeister. "Okay, carry on," he said. The Seaforths and Edmontons would have to soldier on and pay in blood for the important objective.

* * *

Ortona was important. At least in the world press. "Little Stalingrad," the Allied reporters called it. Stories of the hard fighting were appearing on front pages in Canada, Britain and the United States. BBC and CBC radio carried regular updates.

"The English have made it appear as important as Rome," Field Marshal Kesselring complained. "You can do nothing…when the world press makes so much of it."

His Tenth Army commander replied, "It costs so much blood that it cannot be justified."

But the Germans were not going to quit Ortona until forced to do so. Adolf Hitler had taken an interest. He ordered the town held to the last man. But the paratroopers had no intention of obeying. They would fight until it became clear that the battle was lost. Then they would pull out. That time had not come, although many sensed it was not far off.

"The enemy has the major part of the city in his hands," Carl Bayerlein wrote. "With a tremendous barrage the enemy increased his fire. Everywhere there is destruction. The sounds of the engines of the tanks are very close. They advance with the infantry behind.

They seized the hospital...despite our mines and booby traps. We...delay the enemy's advance but we [are] not able to stop him. Our forces are too weak. The outcome is foreseeable."

* * *

That outcome became more certain at 1:00 PM when Lieutenant Colonel Johnston got his Christmas wish. The Highlanders on the ridge were losing a desperate fight that was becoming hand-to-hand. Suddenly Johnston heard the low growl of tank engines and the grinding clank of tracks. Johnston saw his intelligence officer walking toward him on the narrow track the Highlanders had taken to reach the ridge. Rumbling along behind was a Sherman. Its turret turned this way and that, like a dog sniffing the air for the scent of prey. Johnston not only had his Christmas present. He had it three times over. He saw three Shermans grinding along in single file.

They rolled into the shrinking Highlander circle. And started killing. It took only a few minutes and the paratroopers fled. The Highlander position on the ridge was secure.

This was the beginning of the German breakdown. During the night of December 26 their reports of Canadian strength lost all semblance of reality. The three tanks were inflated to sixteen.

Bayerlein wrote that the paratroopers in Ortona faced eight times as many Canadians. His commanders reported even more extreme numbers. Yet together the Edmontons and Seaforths fielded no more than three hundred men. Men so worn out they could barely fight.

CHAPTER SIXTEEN

C BC reporter Matthew Halton recorded a news report on Ortona during the morning. "An epic thing is happening amid the crumbling and burning walls. For seven days and seven nights the Canadians have been trying to clear the town. And the action is as fierce as perhaps modern man has ever fought. For seven days and seven nights the Canadians have been attacking in Ortona. Yard by yard, building by building, window by window. And for seven days and seven nights the sullen young zealots of a crack German parachute division have been defending like demons.

"Canadian and German seem to be both beyond exhaustion and beyond fear. The battle has the quality of a nightmare. Like the fight at Stalingrad. The same apocalyptic pall of smoke and fire and maniacal determination. The splitting steel storm never stops and the men in there are as if possessed. Wounded men refuse to leave and the men don't want to be relieved after seven days and seven nights."

The Canadians, Halton declared, "have asked not to be relieved, and deeds that have been done there will add selfless courage to the heritage of all men...For us at least there is nothing but Ortona today. The infantry and tanks fight from yard to yard with all the more stubbornness after the seven days and seven nights."

* * *

High explosives became the weapon of choice on December 27. Canadian artillery slammed down throughout the German sector.

The Germans responded by dynamiting entire rows of houses. Buildings collapsed and streets filled with rubble. Fires burned out of control throughout the town. Choking smoke drifted like fog through it.

The Canadians kept pressing forward. The Germans were being squeezed into an ever-shrinking corner. They were running out of room to move. Carl Bayerlein, Fritz Illi and the rest prayed for orders to leave. Their units had been shredded. More men were dead than alive. No more reinforcements were being sent in. The survivors fought on in despair, fearing that Hitler would demand they die here. Surely their commanders would not let that happen. They must live to fight tomorrow.

* * *

A platoon of twenty-four Eddies captured a large building near the cathedral at dawn. Moments later a massive explosion collapsed it. The battalion's pioneers started digging frantically for survivors, only to be driven off by paratroopers throwing stick grenades from a nearby building. Private G.E. O'Neill charged the German position alone. He cleared the building single-handed.

Four injured men and one corpse were soon rescued. The pioneers kept digging for the remaining nineteen. Rescue efforts would not end until December 30. Only one man, Lance Corporal Roy Boyd, would be found alive.

Word spread that the building had been deliberately collapsed on the platoon. The Eddies decided to retaliate in kind. A nearby building was strongly held by paratroopers. Several pioneers crawled into the basement under it. They spent thirty minutes planting explosive charges. The building was then destroyed. About forty Germans were crushed to death.

* * *

In the schoolhouse ruins, Gordon Currie-Smith lay buried deep in the rubble where he had been since Christmas Eve. He could breathe with difficulty and move his head only slightly. Nothing else was possible. He was no longer thirsty or hungry. Currie-Smith had accepted that the rubble pile would be his tomb.

Yet now, he heard voices. They seemed far away. But they were voices speaking English. Currie-Smith let out a soft croaking sound. It was meant to be a cry for help. He paused. Forced himself to breathe deeply and work up a little saliva. Then he yelled. He yelled as loudly as possible. Then he yelled again. He kept on yelling until he heard sounds directly above him.

Currie-Smith called out his own name. He listened to the sounds of the shovels and picks working in the rubble. Suddenly the large concrete slab above him was pulled aside. Two men gently lifted him onto a stretcher. His ordeal was over and Currie-Smith was too happy to speak. He would spend the rest of the war recovering from his injuries.

* * *

Ortona's ordeal was also coming to an end. The German High Command decided at 11:00 AM that the battle was lost. Hitler's orders were ignored. The paratroopers were directed to withdraw that night.

There was no letup in the fighting. No hint to the Canadians that the end was near.

Carl Bayerlein and the other engineers blew up more buildings that afternoon than ever. They stopped the destruction only when the last dynamite had been used. Paratroopers fought fanatically to hold on to every building they didn't destroy.

* * *

Brigadier Hoffmeister visited the Seaforth battalion headquarters in the afternoon. Lieutenant Colonel Thomson looked like all of his men. His weight had dropped to 140 pounds. His face was lined and gaunt. He sagged with exhaustion. Thomson told

Hoffmeister that only rum kept him going. The brigadier patted him on the back. "Great show, Syd, terrific show. You are doing great." Thomson smiled wanly. He bit back a plea to be allowed a rest. He and his men must soldier on.

Hoffmeister realized it was time to commit the brigade's remaining battalion. He would send the Princess Patricia's into the fight the next morning. They could move in between the Seaforths and Eddies, fight through to the castle and finish the job. The time was right. He sensed the paratroopers were ready to collapse. Another hard push would do it.

* * *

Night wrapped the ruins of Ortona in a dark cloak. The Canadians stopped advancing. They waited for the dawn. It seemed the Germans did likewise. There was little shooting, few grenades thrown.

The Canadians had no idea the Germans were leaving. The paratroopers disappeared like ghosts into the darkness. Fritz Illi and his men gathered up their weapons. Then they walked away without a backward glance. They marched out of the town and up a road that led north. They marched toward a new position on the north bank of the Arielli River. They would dig in there and fight again.

Bayerlein later wrote in his diary: *There is no town left. Only the ruins. In the evening at 2200 hours we left without making noise. The enemy did not realize this. We left with all our weapons. I had only five rounds of ammunition. The enemy gained a destroyed city. We left undefeated.*

* * *

Ortona woke to an eerie calm on December 28. Lieutenant Alon Johnson and two men crept out into no man's land. He soon heard excited voices speaking Italian. They moved forward through the rubble and battered buildings.

133

He and the men took what cover they could as they searched for the source of the ever-louder chatter.

They found a group of civilians standing in a street. More were coming out of cellars. A young Italian who spoke English guided Johnson to a building. It had been the German headquarters. The building was empty. Johnson realized the paratroopers were gone. "I can't understand what took you so long," the Italian said. "There weren't that many Germans."

Johnson bit back a sharp retort. The young man had no idea what he was talking about. He had never fought. He had never seen so many friends die. His opinion didn't matter. All that mattered was that the Battle of Ortona was over.

CHAPTER SEVENTEEN

Canadian soldiers wandered Ortona's streets in a daze. Some sat down, kicked off broken boots, leaned back and slept like the dead.

CBC war correspondent Matthew Halton later reported, "I went slowly down another main street and came to another square. The buildings were empty shells or piles of brick and rubble, some covered with German dead and blood. And this havoc caused by shells, not bombs. On one pile of rubble, precariously balanced...was a Canadian tank. I see it now as I speak, as I always will see it—not static and dead, but dynamic in that minute when gallantly it climbed the mine-filled pile of rubble only yesterday and was struck down."

The tank was *Amazing*. Joe Turnbull had been rescued from his hiding place in the cellar the day before. He spent all of December 28 searching for his brothers. Finally he found Gord sitting in a shell hole. Gord was staring into space and softly singing "Happy Birthday." Joe went down and sat beside him. Gord stopped singing. Neither man spoke. They just sat together in silent companionship.

In another part of Ortona, Eddies and Seaforths worked frantically to rescue a woman buried inside a destroyed house. Soon they pulled her free. She was pregnant and had gone into labor. A sergeant from Vancouver helped with the delivery. Both mother and child were healthy and well. The woman promised the men her son's middle name would be *Canadese*—Italian for Canadian.

All the Canadians who died in December 1943 were buried in a cemetery south of the town. They numbered 502. Another 1,837 were wounded during this month. Sickness further reduced the division by 1,617 men. Almost 4,000 men out of its total strength of 18,000 became casualties during that month of hell. The Germans suffered similarly heavy casualties.

In Ortona itself the Canadians lost 115 men killed and about 200 wounded. The Germans left behind 200 dead. Ortona's population suffered far more. About 1,300 of its 10,000 residents and refugees died.

The German withdrawal on December 28 did not bring peace to Ortona. They went only a few miles north. Their artillery continued to shell the town in fitful bursts for almost six months. This contributed to the high civilian casualty rate.

Those who survived the Battle of Ortona remembered it for what it was: one of the most epic battles Canada ever fought.

With more than twenty books to his credit, **MARK ZUEHLKE** has been hailed as Canada's leading popular military historian. He is also an award-winning mystery writer. Among the honors his work has received are the Lela Common History Award, the Arthur Ellis Award and the City of Victoria Butler Book Prize. Mark lives in Victoria, British Columbia.